*The Prayer God Answers*

# The Prayer God Answers

Eberhard Arnold & Richard J. Foster

PLOUGH PUBLISHING HOUSE

Published by Plough Publishing House
Walden, New York
Robertsbridge, England
Elsmore, Australia
www.plough.com

ISBN: 978-0-87486-700-8
19  18  17  16  15      2  3  4  5  6  7

Eberhard Arnold's essay was first published in German in 1913 as "Die Übermacht des Gebetslebens" in *Lebensbeweise lebendiger Gemeinden* and revised by the author in 1929. Translated into English by Eileen Robertshaw, Winifred Hildel, and Miriam Mathis; revised and modernized by Charles E. Moore.

Richard J. Foster essay copyright © 2016 by The Richard J. Foster LLC.

Cover image: Vasilij Ivanovic Surikov, detail, *Young Woman at Prayer,* 1879 (oil on canvas). Private Collection / Photo © Bonhams, London, UK / Bridgeman Images

A catalog record for this book is available from the British Library.
Library of Congress Cataloging-in-Publication Data
The prayer God answers / Eberhard Arnold & Richard J. Foster.
    pages cm
  "Eberhard Arnold's essay was first published in German in 1913 as "Die Übermacht des Gebetslebens" in Lebensbeweise lebendiger Gemeinden and revised by the author in 1929. Translated into English by Eileen Robertshaw, Winifred Hildel, and Miriam Mathis; revised and modernized by Charles E. Moore.
  ISBN 978-0-87486-700-8 (pbk.)
  1. Prayer--Christianity. 2. Arnold, Eberhard, 1883-1935. Übermacht des Gebetslebens. I. Arnold, Eberhard, 1883-1935. Übermacht des Gebetslebens. English. II. Foster, Richard J. Perpetual flame of devotion.
  BV210.3.P733 2016
  248.3'2--dc23
                          2015032721

PRINTED IN THE USA

Let anyone who is thirsty come to me and drink.
Whoever believes in me, as Scripture has said, rivers of
living water will flow from within them.

*John 7:37–38*

# *Contents*

# The Prayer God Answers

Eberhard Arnold

# *Why Pray?*

GOD IS LIFE, rich and overflowing life. He is love, and he wants to draw all of us into his life and into his love. Time and again he seeks to lift us into the realm where his life rules.

This is why God stepped out of himself to come to us in his Son. In Jesus, God has opened his heart to us. He has turned his face to us. He comes to us, reveals his thoughts, and shows us who he is and what he wills. He gives us everything we need, and wants to perfect the work he has begun in us. Amazingly, we feeble and insignificant beings are the object of his concern. Out of the incomprehensible love of his heart, God loves each of us quite personally. In his concern for humankind, God seeks out all people and invites them to take part in his new creation.

God wants each of us to respond to him personally and practically. He wants us to know his heart, accept his work, affirm his will, and carry it out. But most of all, God wants to give himself to us. He gives us his spirit so that we might live, act, and work just as his Word did when it became flesh.

God wants us to worship him in the spirit of devotion that grasps the essential and puts it into practice (Matt. 4:10). Since Jesus came to us, we can approach the Father in spirit and in truth (John 4:23–24). The spirit of truth frees us from religious superficiality, idolatry, and impure motives, and brings us under God's rulership. This truth is the clear, authentic Word of God, which has come from God since the beginning of time.

We cannot come to the Father in spirit or in truth if we expend all our strength trying to secure our own salvation, or just keeping our spiritual life above water. People who are so preoccupied with themselves have no strength left to love. But once they are saved from the living death of a separate and selfish life, they will share in the rejuvenating unity and freedom that God promises everyone who is ready to receive Jesus (John 5:24). When they find this freedom, they will devote all they are and have to the One who freed them, giving themselves in love to all people (1 John 3:14). This all-embracing love for others is the mark of those who have an ardent, personal love for Jesus.

THIS PERSONAL LOVE for Jesus finds natural expression in heartfelt prayer. Of course, it is really God whom we love in Christ. If we believe in God as he is, as he lives and works, we shall feel compelled to communicate with him again and again. Those who have faith are filled with unending joy that God can be found now, today.

Through the life, ministry, and death of Jesus, we experience how great and holy God's love is. Because of this we are always conscious of what separates us and cuts us off from the unity which alone can sustain life. We come before God in prayer to confess the separating sin of our own nature, and to thank God for forgiving our sin (Ps. 32:3–6). Christ's victory over sin, evil, and the demonic powers of self unites us with God and with his church.

When we experience the death of Christ, our hearts are made pure. Through community in the church, we are released from the guilt of our egoistic lives. Now we can approach God in complete confidence, our hearts intent on him and his kingdom. We know that the baptism of faith has cleansed us of deadly lust. Bound with others, we live in the certainty of eternal life; we know we can trust in God's faithfulness to his promises (Heb. 10:22–23). And so our hearts overflow with indescribable thankfulness. We cannot help but pray to the One who has delivered us from the blinding darkness, from the sinister spell of Satan's tyranny, and from the body's death and disintegration (Col. 1:12–14).

With great joy we come before God in faith to praise and thank him. We recognize in such experiences that the whole nature and character of God is goodness, kindness, mercy, abundant life, and strengthening love. Our joy in the heart of God moves us to break out in thanksgiving, and our voices ring out, glorifying God in word and song. Instead of plunging us into the wildness and frivolity of selfish enjoyment, our joy leads us to honor God day and night, glorifying him and him alone.

We pray to thank God for all that he is, in the name of Jesus Christ, who revealed him to us. How indescribably great is the love of God, that he is willing to hear, and even desires, this stammering of us feeble human beings! With his light upon us, our joy in thanking him is anchored deeply in what is profoundly serious. We cannot help but honor the untouchable holiness of God and his justice.

Our gratitude can know no bounds. If we really want to honor God, we will also thank him with all our hearts when his just and holy judgment has to humble us and make us small. We will never stand before God demanding, seeking to be justified, or in self-confidence. When we recognize how weak we are and that God loves us and accepts us in our small-ness, the humility of gratitude and worship gives us the courage to speak to God. In fact, we can only pray when we are so keenly aware of our own limitations that it is clear to us that we can do nothing without the power of God's love. We pray to confess our inad-equacy, to admit that God's kingdom is not here, but that we need it and want it to come. We approach God with empty hands. We raise them up and open them to him, and kneel before him to express our smallness and emptiness.

Only through faith in God can his will be fulfilled in our lives. With everything we do, we thank God for giving us a faith that leads to action. Our grati-tude is born of our recognition that we are unworthy of God's care and his generous gifts. It is only through grace that we can do the works of God. Our faith in his unmerited generosity fills us with love, with its insistence on action. When this happens, we come to know what an inexhaustible wealth of grace awaits all those who call on the Lord for power and new life

(Ps. 86:5; Rom. 10:12). We know that this is a power we can never attain on our own. This drives us to pray.

GOD DOES NOT WANT, for his own sake, to be asked that his name be holy, his will good, or his rulership complete. But for our sake he wants us to pray to him for these things, so that instead of profaning his name, resisting his will, and arrogantly asserting ourselves in rebellion against his rule, we might truly revere him, do his will, and accept his rule. He wants us to acknowledge this. He wants us to pray, humbly admitting that our own sinfulness, stubbornness, and halfheartedness are obstacles that only he can overcome.

God is waiting for us to thank him for being willing to arm us with the gift of his spirit. He is waiting for our prayer telling him that if it depended on us, the kingdom of God could not be expected at all; it would be impossible. Actually, God's kingdom does not depend on our praying, our preaching, or our spiritual reading. But only when he is persistently asked will he come and act, for this calling on God is the only way to express the faith that God is God and that he alone can give us what is good.

## The Nature of True Prayer

PRAYER IS NOT MERELY, as some say, "the breathing of the soul." It is the imbibing of life itself. If we stop praying, life ebbs away. As long as we pray, our lives remain warm, ardent, and vigorous, for in prayer we meet God himself in Christ. In Christ is life – yes, in him alone (John 1:4). We experience this life only insofar as we search for him and love him, and only to the extent that we come to him and receive him in prayer. "Eating the flesh" and "drinking the blood" of the Son of Man actually takes place every time we meet him personally, so that he is in us and we are in him. Neither my prayer nor my conduct can bring life; what is crucial is that Christ is my life.

If anyone thinks that prayer is the inner depth of his own conscience, a concentrated monologue of his soul seeking something better, he is still far from true prayer and influenced by all-too-human ideas. Such a person is still outside the gates or perhaps standing on the threshold; he cannot remain there and hope to meet God. He has not yet passed through the holy place of inner surrender, where self and everything belonging to self is given up – even the deep emotions of his own soul. He has not gone into the Holy of Holies where God himself, who is completely other than us and high above even his angel-princes, wants us to call on him. This is the starting point of prayer: the crucial recognition that God is completely different than even the most consecrated and concentrated of our own inner states. In the presence of the infinite goodness and love of God, the clear difference between us and God is revealed.

Someone once compared our relationship to God with a moth that flies around a scorching flame until it is finally burnt up. Prayer in the spirit of Christ is not like this. It is not a matter of the "I" being consumed, but one of a relationship between the small "I" of my spirit and the great "I" of his spirit, so that through meeting God our souls are awakened and made capable of living.

It is true that faith is born in the inmost depth of our soul, rising from there until it governs all our actions. God himself seeks to encounter our spirit in our inner being. There God reveals himself to us as our Father, and accepts as his children those who accept him. We are indeed his children if we can call him "Father." But God is still God, even though he gives us everything, and we are still human, even as children of God. We do not become gods; if we did, we would drive God away.

God sent his Word to become one of us. Jesus alone is uniquely God's son, eternally abiding with God, honoring God as God and as his Father. The Son is so completely one with the Father and the Spirit that one of them cannot exist or work without the others. This puts all of us, including those who have faith, in a definite place, clearly assigned to us. Through Jesus Christ, God brings us to the place that is to remain ours: we do not become more than true people of God, nor more than an image of God. As children of God in this sense, we have faith in him, worship him, and call for him to come.

Faith is the knowledge that God's loving will is to establish justice, holiness, unity, and community. This will abides in him; it is a part of himself. For God is what he is. Christ remains the same yesterday (before time began), today, and through all eternity. That can never be changed. Through faith we know that God, as spirit and love and power, has sought us out and given us a task. He has chosen us weak people to make his name, his will, and his rulership known far and wide on this earth.

Prayer is thus an act of faith. We cannot call on God, we cannot appeal to his nature, if we do not believe in him as he actually is. No one can pray unless the Holy Spirit has led him to faith in God. Unless the Spirit has brought our hearts and lives under the rule of Christ, it is hypocrisy for us to call on God as Lord and Master. Without the Holy Spirit there is no prayer in faith. There is not even faith.

God gives himself to us as the Holy Spirit. Only in this spirit can we do his will and carry out his work. The kingdom of God – with its justice, peace, joy, brotherhood, unity, and love – is given to us through the Holy Spirit. If we desire these gifts, we should ask for the Holy Spirit to take possession of our hearts, remold our lives, and lead us to the true church. God's kingdom can become a reality here and now if we but entrust ourselves to this spirit: the spirit of discipline and love, the spirit that overcomes sin and glorifies Christ, the spirit of Jesus' words, of the church, and of God's future.

God in his goodness has promised to give the Holy Spirit to anyone who earnestly asks him. Jesus himself promised it. Jesus calls on us now (as he called on the

Samaritan woman at the well) to ask him for this spring of living, streaming water (John 4:10). We are to ask in expectation and trust that this spring will never be brackish or stagnant and will never run dry. Only in this river of the Spirit, flowing full of God's power, can faith live. Away from this river it dies like a fish on dry land.

Just as Jesus prayed that Peter's faith should never run dry (Luke 22:32), so he prayed expressly for us who later would believe through the words of his apostles (John 17:20). God gives his Spirit to all who love him and do his will, just as Jesus asked in his prayer. The Spirit makes Jesus alive in them and gives them his faith, so that their prayer is no different from his.

Therefore, when we pray, let us remember that God in his Spirit approaches and calls us first. Only then may we call him by his name. When we call on him in this way, after God has spoken to us, we will be saved. If we search for him with all our hearts, he lets us find him with absolute certainty, because he already searched for us and called to us when we had forgotten him entirely.

For this reason, prayer is first listening to God. Once we listen, then we can speak to him. If we want to enter into community with God, we must hear what he is saying and ask for his Spirit and his Word. To speak God's living word into our hearts, the Spirit uses people who teach the truth and proclaim the message that frees us, telling us who God is, what he wants, and what he has done and is doing (Rom. 10:13–17). That is why the church has taken care to preserve the divine revelations of the great eras of God's history: the living words spoken by God through the prophets and apostles, through the writings of people of God, and through the eternally living martyrs.

NOT ONLY INDIVIDUALS, but every church and fellowship that hopes to discover powerful, united prayer first needs to practice silence, for it is important that we learn to recognize what God wishes to say. We must perceive his voice in the events around us and in our own midst. We must hear his voice in our hearts. And in the midst of all the darkness that blights the earth today, we must look to his light, the light of the rising morning star, the light of the coming day, which is prepared by God and which no one can bring about. We must discover the light that shines for every human being who is born into this world, through the One who came into this world as the son of Mary, as the light of the world. And we will only learn to call on God in prayer and to thank him when we have learned to hear him.

Before we speak to him, God must have spoken to us. And he always speaks. His Word is always active. But we do not always perceive it. This is why we need to be quiet in the depths of our souls, where we hear his voice and see his light. When we do this, we will experience something wonderful. We will find that Jesus Christ is the same in times gone by, now, and in the time to come, the time of his future kingdom. We will find that he is the same for all people, that he has the same will, the same way, the same truth, and the same love for all. And we will learn that the voice of the Holy Spirit says the same thing to each of us.

God is called "I am who I am." His will does not bend. He does not conform to certain things or certain people. He remains unchangeable. We will experience this when we truly learn to listen to the Spirit, when we hearken to the wind that comes to us from God. Meeting in silence, we will hear the same voice and perceive the same truth. Through silence, we will become united in heart and voice.

WE HUMANS, SO far from God and estranged from the truth, should remember that the Holy Spirit, full of light, warmth, and power, brings our prayer before God in his pure heights far above us. There the revelations stream out like light, while we, sunk in the twilight of our human condition, grope in vain for a clear thought or word. Still, we groan and sigh in longing for God because we cannot live without him – because we want to love and honor him, but do not even know how.

When we sincerely ask God for his Spirit, he comes and speaks and acts (Acts 4:31, 8:15–17). His divine energy is always present, ready to strike like lightning. But the only ground into which it can discharge its power is our humble, concentrated readiness in prayer.

When we are ready in this sense we can experience prayer to a point of ecstasy that transports us into God's world. The shining Spirit never leaves us in the fading light of unclarity when we have prayed to receive its light. But it is better to pray clearly and intelligibly in the Spirit than to pray in ecstatic tongues that cannot be understood (1 Cor. 14:13–19). Paul prays for the Philippians that their love may abound in knowledge and clear discernment of what is right and fitting (Phil. 1:9–10). We too are to ask for wisdom and discernment, and to ask in childlike faith, without the emotional uncertainty of inflated self-esteem or a heart divided by desire for our own satisfaction.

GOD'S LIFE SWEEPS AWAY all phony, dull piety. In the Lord's Prayer, Jesus opposes the boastful utterance, which calls for admiration; the long-winded prayer, which gratifies our ego more the longer it is; and the self-concerned, emotional prayer, which puts feelings in the place of God (Matt. 6:5–7). Jesus told his disciples that they were not to pray as most people do, thinking their prayers will be answered if they use big words and pray for a long time. He had already shown them that they should be brief and clear in speaking with people, with the plain truthfulness which says yes when it means yes and no when it means no. They were to speak with God in the same way.

The example that comes down to us from the men of old shows us what it means to approach God. For these men, the only thing that mattered was God – his honor, his spirit, his clarity, and the coming of his Messiah. The unbroken thread of prayer, the story of a clearly defined relationship with the living God, runs from Abraham, Isaac, and Jacob, through Moses, Joshua, Gideon, Samson, and Job, through Samuel,

Elijah, and Elisha, through David and Hezekiah, to Isaiah, Jeremiah, and the other prophets. For them, as for us today, it was only because of a definite promise from God, and only when they really wanted something, that they could gather courage to ask. Their prayers were straightforward and practical: they prayed for the needs of their people, for their king, and ultimately for the kingdom of God. Because God had given them clear and unmistakable promises, they could bring forward simple, definite requests. They could remind God that he had given them his word. They knew what God's will was; that is why God did as they asked when they prayed to him.

## *Does God Hear Us?*

IN THE DAYS OF OLD, there were also people who complained that their prayer remained unanswered (Lam. 3:8, 44), just as it does today whenever we come to God expecting him to support our selfish purposes, demanding our rights, and purposely ignoring his will. On the other hand, the Old Testament is full of stories that show that God never rejects the prayers of people who are surrendered to him in faith. In every case, he allowed their cry to reach his great, strong heart. He heard it. He accepted it. He rejoiced that in their faith they thought of him as inclining his ear to them, turning toward them to see and hear them as they called to him.

The prayers of believers rise up like incense. They are truly present around the throne of God. As long as the work and activity of our practical life are at one with God's will, our true and heartfelt prayer comes right into God's presence (Acts 10:4). It reaches his heart, which is waiting and longing for our will at last to declare its agreement with his will. Then God immediately gives his answer: Your prayer has been heard! (Luke 1:13, Acts 10:31).

GOD IS ALWAYS NEAR, ready to listen to his people whenever they pray in accordance with his will. He is, to put it in other words, very close to us when we are so deeply in trouble that we have stopped looking for help from our own efforts or from any human source. He is near, very near, when we truly pray for nothing but the honor of his name, and ask for nothing but his intervention, his fire, his rain, the shining, streaming energy of his love. When the object of our prayer accords with God's will and the prayer is made without hypocrisy, with undeviating and complete honesty, then it is in harmony with God's power. God listens to the spirit of God.

Jesus tells us that God wants to know what our will is. He wants to know the desire of our heart. But the words we use should be nothing more nor less than a declaration that we are ready for his will to be done and for his kingdom to come on this earth. We should ask God as clearly and simply as possible that his nature may be revealed, that is, that his will is done in our lives so that it becomes clear to all who God truly is.

I have heard people say, "At one time I was very near to God, but he didn't answer my prayers. Since then I haven't been so sure about him." Such people fail to realize that God may have wanted to say something to them through this, namely, that none of us really knows what to pray for or what is best for us. If we want to give God orders, if we want to dictate God's direction through our prayers, then such prayers are not under the blessing of God. Rather, these prayers are born of the spirit of darkness, the spirit that told Eve, "You shall be like God."

True prayer acknowledges that of ourselves we are incapable of striking the right course in prayer. True prayer demands complete surrender and complete confidence, so that we can say, "We do not know what we ought to pray for, but the Spirit himself intercedes for us with groans that words cannot express" (Rom. 8:26–30).

When we come before God, we do not always find the right words. We are often unclear about what we want to pray for. We are sometimes so weak we cannot even gather our thoughts sufficiently to frame our prayer in words at all. Yet there is one who knows everything that is in our hearts. If we know him, then we will say with Peter, "Lord, you know all things. You know that I love you" (John 21:15–17).

It can also happen that we are so overwhelmed with God's presence that we are only capable of an unutterable sighing of the soul. Such an experience makes us conscious of our weakness. We feel how pitiable the vessel of our body is for the superabundant revelation of God.

Teresa of Avila, the Catholic saint, compared the soul with a garden. This garden must be watered. There are rare times in which the life of the soul is flooded with streams of the Spirit, in which the whole garden is so well watered that one cannot find a dry place anywhere, and for a long period the garden blossoms and bears fruit. On the other hand, there also come times in which we wring out our prayers, just as one squeezes the last drop out of something.

OUR PRAYERS will be answered under these conditions: that we pray for God's honor and the glory of his name; that we ask for the stamp of his character on human life and the faithful portrayal of his likeness; that we pray that his church truly embodies Christ;

and that we ask for the practical, communal fulfillment of his will in unity and harmony with his Spirit
and in the faith that does the works of love. That is
the meaning, hidden to most, of the well-known yet
mysterious words of Jesus: "I will do whatever you
ask in my name" (John 14:13–14). The substance of
our prayer, what we are asking God to bring about,
is none other than that which God already wants. He
has simply been waiting until we are ready. And our
readiness is proved by the genuineness of our prayer.

God is always ready. With the intensity of his holy
will, he longs for people of faith to speak, pray, live,
and believe so completely in the living Jesus that he
is at last able to intervene and act as he has always
wanted to act. In answer to our faith, and to the
measure of our faith, everything will be done just as
we ask. There is no wall, no mountain, no barrier too
high for the prayer of faith.

When we live and pray as Jesus did, then like
him we can have the complete confidence that the
Father has heard us, even while we are still praying
(John 11:41). The power and authority that God has
given his people lies in this unity with Jesus; our life,
our longing, and our prayer must be united with
his. In the midst of healing the sick and driving out

demons, Jesus called to God, "Father, I thank you for answering my prayer." For him, communion with God was an event, a breaking in of eternal powers, a happening that brought with it mighty consequences. Every time we come to God in Jesus' name, heaven will open above us as it opened when Jesus prayed at his baptism (Luke 3:21). But this will never happen unless we live the way Jesus lived, in poverty and readiness to suffer as he did.

Like Jesus, we must be ready to accept dire poverty and a bitter death. Unless we endure his suffering and share his anguish, we will never be able to share his glory. We can never share in the power of his resurrection and the world to come unless we can drink his cup of death ourselves (Matt. 20:22). Like Jesus in Gethsemane, we must accept the cup with all its blood and agony, in complete readiness to die, so that the Father's will may be done. Like Jesus on the cross, we must be ready to suffer godforsakenness, yet still pray trustingly, "Father, into your hands I commit my spirit!" (Luke 23:46).

Francis of Assisi showed the people of his time, as Jesus' true followers in every age have shown, that real joy is not to be found in exalted feelings, or in knowledge and prophecy, or in converting others. We can find perfect joy only when we suffer cold and hunger and are rejected, beaten, and derided for representing Christ's love and humility – only when we endure the cross with a kind and cheerful heart.

Even in his group of wandering brothers, Francis found that Christ sometimes let himself be sought in great anxiety for many days. We, too, must seek him intensely and in distress until he at last enfolds us in his arms and fills us with the glowing breath of his love. The sixteenth-century Anabaptist Peter Riedemann writes:

> The person who prays in faith never ceases to make his request to God and allows no other concern to hinder him. If there should be a delay and it seems as though God will not grant his request, he waits patiently, in confidence that God will surely respond soon. Those who, after they have prayed, immediately turn their attention to something else and are distracted from their request, and those who stop praying because they get tired of asking, can receive nothing.

We cannot ask effectively for different things at the same time. We must pray for one definite object. Our prayer also cannot be effective without the most ardent longing. But this longing must arise from the right motives. There must be no selfishness behind it. If our motives are pure, we will persevere until we are heard, with constant sighing and yearning and with a concentration of all the powers of the soul – a real wrestling with God "with loud cries and tears" (Heb. 5:7).

If it is the consequence of real love and real conviction, the intense longing of such prayer deeply unites Jesus and his people; they come to understand the intensity of God's longing for the salvation of the sinner. In this way it also unites them with the unconverted through the power of love.

God arouses the longing in us that he wants to still. Therefore, the faintest longing must be carefully nursed. If we let ourselves be filled with the Holy Spirit, there will be no lack of thirst, nor will our prayer lack focus. Do not dampen the Spirit! Do not turn your thoughts to other things!

In his parables, Jesus suggests that our prayer will not be heard unless we persist with this urgent desire, even to the point of suffering. The widow had to bring her plea to the judge over and over again before he finally granted her request (Luke 18:1–8). The man who went at night to ask his friend for bread dared to knock again and again until his friend at last got out of bed and gave him what he wanted (Luke 11:5–8). God sometimes waits till we have reached a state of utter distress and destitution to see if we are really in earnest and want only what he wants. If we are not going to succumb under the pressures of such a needy state, we must remain on watch the whole time and pray with ever-increasing urgency (Luke 21:36). Then our prayers will be answered.

## Obstacles to Prayer

EVEN THOUGH WE ALL LONG for the kingdom of God – for unity with God and for the total dominion of the Holy Spirit over all other spirits – we know that we are obstacles to this kingdom. Our own nature is always interfering when God tries to reveal himself. Our personalities get in the way, because in each of us there are countless thoughts, feelings, and traits of character that are not completely centered on the kingdom of God or compatible with the spirit of Jesus. Every prayer is therefore inevitably burdened with personal mistakes and desires.

In addition to our own failings, we are often besieged by dark clouds of worry. When this happens we need to ask for the freshening wind of the Holy Spirit so that, surrounded by God's pure, clear atmosphere, we can pray tirelessly to God, asking him to banish our anxiety and prove that he is the ruler over life and death. By praying we can resist temptation (Matt. 26:41).

Even more dangerous than the most nightmarish anxiety is the force that drives away the Spirit: sin. Sin fights against life and leads to death through the demonic darkness of unrighteousness, impurity, covetousness, self-will, and deception.

These demonic forces will yield only to prayer offered in a spirit of self-denying love. Sin and the prayer of faith exclude each other. We cannot meet God unless we are free from hate, anger, quarreling, and all wrong done to others (1 Tim. 2:8). If we are serious about praying we must be cleansed of all sin. God dwells only in hearts that have been completely purified. We cannot speak to God, who is holy, unless we have prayed for the forgiveness of our sins with a converted and changed heart, and truly believe in and live in this forgiveness.

"Everyone who confesses the name of the Lord must turn away from wickedness" (2 Tim. 2:19). That is the clear stamp by which God can recognize his own. If we refuse to listen to God's demands for righteousness, our prayer is an abomination. It is loathsome to God. As long as we continue to shed the blood of others, none of our prayers will be heard. With all the strength and determination we can muster, we must reject evil and strive to do only what is good. We must try to show justice and love to all people, especially to the poor and deserted, the widows and orphans. We must be ready to fulfill the will of God with the willing obedience of faith. Only then will God take away our sins and accept our prayers.

Unless we have utterly surrendered ourselves to God and left behind all selfishness, our prayer for God's gifts will have no effect (James 4:2–3). Everything, absolutely everything, that stifles our love for him must be burned away.

The sin that separates us from God most is the cold arrogance of a self-centered, individualistic life. The key to prayer is to give up all the privileges, rights, and demands of self-esteem, all self-justification, and all clinging to the good things we have accomplished through our own virtue. Self-importance is the opposite of love and goodness and is the deepest root of sin. Conversely, the root of community with God and love to others is the awareness that we receive undeserved grace and good gifts from God. If we are full of ourselves, thinking we are better than others, our prayer will never reach God. But if we are aware of our guilt and recognize that we are worse than others, and ask God for his mercy, he accepts our prayers (Luke 18:9–14).

Our prayers are blocked whenever our hearts remain unmoved. To experience a fundamental change of heart and direction and to enter a new life in God, we must first feel profound remorse for the heartless evil of our self-governed lives. People who see their guilt as it really is learn through God's judgment to detest sin and to turn away from it forever. They spend the rest of their lives in awe before God, for now they know that the Father to whom they pray is no respecter of persons but judges all of us according to our actions, and that the purpose of his judgment is to destroy what is evil in us. When we have been overpowered by God in this way, we will keep watch in every area of our lives and in all our relationships, particularly in marriage (1 Cor. 7:5). We will not let pleasures, especially those of possession and sensuality, distract us from God and hinder our prayers. Prayer demands clearheaded moderation.

PRAYER IS A POWERFUL WEAPON. But the full power of forgiveness, of the healing laying-on-of-hands, and of prayer dwells only in the united church, in an undivided people fully consecrated to his kingdom. This is why an individual interested only in himself and his own emotional state can never experience the true power of prayer.

When people gather for the kingdom and unite in prayer for forgiveness, in dead earnest, in the knowledge of their own smallness, and in their desire for a complete change of heart, they pray for the welfare of the whole body of believers, for they feel it to be their own welfare. We, too, should always pray for the overcoming of the sickness and sins of the whole church. This will clear away every hindrance to God working in the church. As long as all our sins are confessed, and as long as we as individuals bring our sickness to the church, the prayer of the church has power over sickness and sin.

We must not forget: the individual believer is not the new body of Christ. We as individuals, in all our smallness, may take part in the church of God on this earth; we may reflect, practice, and express the Father's nature in words and life and work. But the church, with the authority given to it by God, is the new embodiment of the Word made flesh.

In praying to God, the ruling, commanding, helping, and loving "Thou," we can overcome the human resistance of our rebellious "I" only through the "we" of the church. In other words, we should never cease praying for our brothers and sisters in Christ, asking that the Spirit may give them true wisdom and insight into the will of God and so lead them to live rightly and do what is good (Col. 1:9–10, Phil. 1:3–9). If we ever slacken in our concern and prayer for our brothers and sisters, we are sinning against God.

Our prayers remain insipid if their primary focus is on our personal needs. Rather, we should pray earnestly night and day that God may take away all shortcomings in the entire church, so that we may rediscover the true and living fellowship that existed in the early church's common life of faith – a practical and spiritual community where believers saw each other daily and were closely united in all matters.

Jesus sent the uniting Spirit to the first Christians with such power that they worshiped him in a faith and love that put true community with God into practice. For them the Spirit and Jesus were one and the same. Jesus had walked among them as a man among men. Now he was living among them through the Spirit. Christ's perfect love had become their life and their love. This love was overflowing fullness of life, which came to expression in community. A private life of even the greatest personal piety can never have this overflowing abundance of God.

God cannot hear us if we are at odds with one another. The Holy Spirit leads all the members of the church to pray for one and the same thing, and when they do, what they ask and long for will happen. United with all people everywhere who call on the Lord with a pure heart, they want only one thing: that God's justice, love, and peace would rule on earth. The unity of their purpose unites them before God and unleashes the power of prayer.

Jesus says, "If two of you on earth agree about anything you ask for, it will be done for you by my Father in heaven" (Matt. 18:19). What matters is not the words we use, especially not the quantity of them. What matters is that we are united in what we ask for. If the church achieves unity in the object of its prayer, there is no need for a great many sentences giving an exact description; God needs no explanation from us. What matters is that when we gather together there is complete agreement as to what we want to ask God for. Only then can we call on him with confidence.

Consider more carefully how the Christians of the early church prayed. They were constantly united in calling on God (Acts 1:14). They could pray in such perfect harmony and truthfulness because their whole way of life was honest from the very foundation, having everything in common, sharing their daily meals and all their goods, and keeping nothing from each other. When the church gave thanks, the "amen" declared the affirmation of the whole gathering, uniting them with all people throughout the world who call on Jesus (1 Cor. 1:2). And from their end, those who lived in other places sent money and gifts to the early church at Jerusalem to support the common life with its self-sacrificing community of goods and hospitality, and to show their thankfulness to God (2 Cor. 9:11–13).

They consecrated the fellowship of their meals by hearing God's Word and by offering him their prayers of thanksgiving, as Jesus had done, and as all people of faith from the earliest times on have done, thanking God for their good health and for what he has done. The one meal consecrated above all others as a time of holy thanksgiving and worship was the communal meal of bread and wine to proclaim and remember the death of Jesus (Matt. 26:26–28).

In all their gatherings, they thanked God and Christ for the Spirit's victories in spreading the truth, and they prayed that the knowledge of Christ would have an ever-stronger influence throughout the world, as did the apostle Paul. They asked God to keep sending new workers to help gather people to the faith, as wheat is gathered at harvest time (Luke 10:2). They knew that apostles sent out on this task should be devoted to prayer and to proclaiming the Word. As Jesus had laid his hands on little children and prayed, they used the laying-on-of-hands as a prayer, especially for their elders and for people being sent out on mission.

In the early church, prayer became a powerful river of life flowing out from a life of brotherhood to the world around it, through the working of the gifts of the Spirit and through mission. It could be the same today. Prayer is, and always will be, the vital nerve of the church.

# Praying for the Kingdom

JESUS AND HIS APOSTLES never taught a theology or a philosophy. They addressed life – actual, practical life. Whoever has faith in Jesus has life (1 John 5:12). Holding fast to the Son of God is no otherworldly matter; it is a concrete reality that translates faith into deeds. "If you remain in me, and my words remain in you, ask whatever you wish, and it will be given you" (John 15:7). These words of Jesus are the life we pray for. They cover everything that can happen to us.

Nothing shows this more clearly than the Lord's Prayer (Matt. 6:9–13). The "Our Father" sums up the message of the gospel, so that in every era, all areas of life can be filled with the fresh and vital life of God. Hence, every prayer offered in the Spirit will ultimately correspond with what is expressed in the Lord's Prayer. It covers everything we human beings need to live as God wants us to live, just as completely as it encompasses the honor of God and his holy will.

Whenever we come before God we should ask for the bread we need, the forgiveness of our sins, protection from temptation, and reconciliation with others. All this belongs to true prayer. But most importantly, we need to ask that God's will is done and that his kingdom comes. Our personal prayers remain selfish unless they are placed in the larger context of God's rulership being established on earth. This is the only way in which we may bring our personal needs before God; they must be placed in the setting of his great and all-inclusive power. We should see these personal requests to God as part of the one object of our prayer: that the Spirit come down and fill us and change everything from the bottom up.

We should be brief and to the point when we ask God for this one, all-important thing. Wordy prayer and lazy prayer – trying to make an impression by reciting prayers instead of doing the will of God – are more heathen than Christian. Clearly, communal prayer has a place in the church; it is equally clear that it cannot be a spectacle for the general public. Besides, the prayer of the church depends on the secluded prayer life of individual believers. Withdrawal into quiet and solitude is one of the most decisive characteristics of Jesus. He retired to the isolated mountain, the lonely wilderness, or the quiet water so he could meet his Father completely alone (Matt.14:23). But days rich in work always preceded and followed these nights when he was alone with God.

PRAYER MUST NEVER SUPPLANT WORK. If we sincerely ask God for his will to be done, for his nature to be revealed in our work, for his rule to bring humankind to unity, justice, and love, then our life will be one of work. Faith without works is dead. Prayer without work is hypocrisy. Unless we actively work to build up God's kingdom, the Lord's Prayer – "Your kingdom come" – is a lie on our lips. The purpose of Jesus' prayer is to bring us to the point where its meaning is lived out, where it actually happens and becomes part of history. Each of us needs to find a way to devote our whole working strength so that God is honored, his will is done, and his kingdom comes. Unless our love for Jesus results in deeds, our connection to the Tree of Life will wither.

In addition, if we are going to endure the weight of evil and suffering in this world, we must not only ask God to forgive our sins, but that he would grant us the love that forgives everyone all the evil they have done to us. When Jesus taught us to pray, he laid down this attitude as a condition. So when we pray, interceding on behalf of others for the sake of God's kingdom, we must pray most of all for those who have hurt us. In his dying agony, Jesus prayed that his torturers be forgiven. We, too, must recognize that our enemies do not always know what they are doing. We must pray, as did Stephen and many other Christian martyrs, that God does not hold our persecutors' sin against them.

Our prayer, therefore, should encompass all people everywhere, from all nations, that they may be united in serving Jesus. It may include our needs, but it should encompass the whole world.

In the end, all nations will be gathered and purified in the fire of God's wrath and zeal; then they will call on him and serve him shoulder to shoulder. This is why Paul thanks God for making us heirs to his future and bringing us into Christ's eternal kingdom (Col. 1:12–14). He knows that the name of the Lord will be glorified through all eternity, and that all creation will be filled with thanksgiving and worship. And so the Lord's Prayer closes in worship, that the kingdom and the power and the glory belong to the Father forever.

If our prayer is genuine, if we really want nothing but the kingdom of God, then we will think of all the regions of the world. We will call on God to intervene in the history of the nations, the history of classes and ranks, the history that has brought injustice to a climax. We will call on him to come with his judgment and to let his righteousness and peace break in like the dawn. This should be our prayer and the prayer of the church.

WHEN WE CALL ON GOD, we are asking him to do something that we cannot, to bring into being something that we ourselves do not know how to create. We are seeking for the impossible to happen, for something to be changed irrevocably that we could never change. We are asking for a history to unfold for which we ourselves could never be responsible.

The question is: Do we have the faith that through our prayer the status quo can be shattered? Can we believe that at our call Christ will come among us to judge and save? When we ask for the Holy Spirit, are we ready for God to strike us like a burst of flaming lightning, so that at last we experience Pentecost? Do we really believe that God's kingdom is imminent? Are we capable of believing that through our pleading this kingdom will break in? Are we able to believe that as a result of our prayer the entire history of the world will be turned topsy-turvy?

Let us come to God in the absolute certainty that Jesus' words are true: "The kingdom of God has drawn near!" and, "If you have faith, nothing will be impossible for you." Wonders will occur, mountains will be torn from their place, and the whole situation as it is on earth will be changed. Mighty things will happen when we have faith.

It is dangerous to call on God in this way, for it means we are ready, not only to be lifted up from our place, but to be hurled down from our place. So let us concentrate all our powers on Jesus' nearness, on the silent coming of the Holy Spirit, ready for everything to be changed by his intervention.

God is above everything. Christ is stronger than all other spirits. When our faith, life, and deeds are in Jesus, all our prayers are answered. If everything we do has only one goal – that his kingdom comes and his will is done on earth – then the things we pray for will happen. God will show us that he is greater than our hearts can grasp. Much more will happen than we could dare put into words. God's answer will surpass our boldest prayer. And so that we know it is

God who does it all, it will happen while we are still praying, or even before we have spoken our prayer. Anyone who knocks at God's door and seeks nothing but God alone will receive what he asks for in the twinkling of an eye.  ✦

# The Perpetual Flame of Devotion

*A reflective response by Richard J. Foster*

## Three Movements of Prayer

*By means of prayer we are learning to burn the per-petual flame of devotion on the altar of God's love. I say "learning" because there is nothing automatic or instantaneous about this way of praying.*

NOW, THREE GREAT MOVEMENTS characterize Christian prayer. Each is distinct from the others but overlaps and interacts with the others.

The first movement in prayer involves *our will in interaction and struggle with God's will.* We ask for what we need – or what we want. Often what we want exceeds what we need, and our wants can be easily influenced by ego and greed. Most certainly, a sub-stantial part of our inner struggle in this movement involves our own human rebellion and self-centered-ness. But not always. Think of Abraham struggling to offer up Isaac. Or think of Job struggling to relin-quish all human attachments. Or think of Paul struggling with a "thorn in the flesh" and learning that God's grace is sufficient for him and that God's power is made perfect in weakness.

So, this first movement in prayer is not to be despised. During this process we are learning the many intimate details of human interaction with our God, who is ever-loving and ever-patient.

In time, we come into a second movement in prayer: *the release of our will and a flowing into the will of the Father.* Here we are learning to walk with God day by day. We are learning the contours of God's character. And we are learning simple love for Jesus.

Finally, we find ourselves entering into the third movement, what the great ones in the way of Christ have called *"union with God" and the bringing of the will of the Father upon the face of the earth.* Here we learn not only to love God, but also to love God's ways. Through experience we come to understand that God's ways are both altogether right and altogether good – we learn the goodness of rightness. Over time we develop a deep rhythm of living that can rest at ease with the cosmic patience of God. Here our mind and heart and spirit increasingly take on the loving character of Christ. In the earlier movements we were learning the multiplied nuances of praying, "Thy will be done." Now, in this third movement, God gladly says to us, "Your will be done!" And to our utter amazement we discover that what we will conforms to the will of God. We are in "union" with the Divine Center, to use the phrase of Thomas Kelly.[1]

## *An Astonishing Ministry*

These three movements in prayer are well expressed and detailed in the life and writings of Eberhard Arnold. His astonishing ministry occurred in Germany between the enormous upheavals of World War I and World War II. His major work, *Innerland,* absorbed his energies for most of his life. The manuscript had to be packed in metal boxes and buried at night for safekeeping from the Nazis, who raided his study on two occasions. *Innerland* spoke forcefully against the demonic spirits that animated German society in that day: the murderous strains of racism and bigotry, the heady nationalistic fervor, the mindless mass hysteria, and the vulgar materialism.

In 1933 the Bruderhof, the intentional Christian community that Arnold had founded, was stormed by the Gestapo, SS, and police and its school was closed. Ultimately the Bruderhof community was forced to flee Nazi oppression, first to Liechtenstein and then to England. Today Bruderhof communities can be found in several countries around the world.

In the midst of this tumultuous era in human history, Arnold penned his lucid and wise essay, *The Prayer God Answers.* In it he traverses the landscape of the three great movements in Christian prayer, providing us vital and hard-won insights into the life of faith.

Arnold begins by addressing the foundational question: Why should we pray in the first place? Next, he helps us understand "the nature of true prayer" before turning to what is perhaps the most pressing practical question for those learning to pray: Does God really hear us when we pray? Arnold then tackles the various obstacles you and I face as we seek to pray day in and day out. He concludes with a cosmic vision of the life of the kingdom of God coming to all peoples everywhere. In the midst of the struggle and suffering that is part of the human condition, he encourages us to walk cheerfully over the earth in the love and power of God.

I believe it would be helpful to follow each of these five salient themes and provide simple commentary upon each of them. Hopefully in this way we will be able to think *with* Eberhard Arnold about "the prayer God answers."

## Why Pray?

Arnold begins his essay with a profoundly basic question about prayer: Why pray? The question is well and good, and instinctively we are looking for the standard answers. Religious obligation perhaps. Or seeking material things. Or desperate personal need. Or even the yearning of the human heart to experience God. These reasons for praying we understand, and even expect.

But right here Arnold turns the whole matter on its head and plunges us into the mystery of God's unfathomable love. The opening paragraph immediately turns us toward this mystery: "God is life, rich and overflowing life. He is love, and he wants to draw all of us into his life and into his love. Time and again he seeks to lift us into the realm where his life rules."

Next, Arnold piles phrase upon phrase to describe this "incomprehensible love of God's heart." He exclaims in utter amazement, "How indescribably great is the love of God!" We bow in doxology, knowing that "the whole nature and character of God is goodness, kindness, mercy, abundant life, and strengthening love."

So we are drawn into prayer not by obligation or by need or by desire but by divine Love. God seeking. God waiting. God wooing. God pursuing. This emphasis upon the loving heart of God seeking us out is, of course, drawing from a long and deep biblical tradition about prayer.

One personal life-altering experience in the summer of 1990 may help to unpack this critical teaching.[2] I was working on a book on prayer. Of course, it wasn't a book then, just thousands of notes scrawled on scraps of paper and napkins and anything else I could find. I didn't even have a title for the book. The library staff at the university where I was teaching at the time had provided me with a room for my research. They had also given me a key to the library building so I could go in anytime, day or night.

Over that summer I had worked in perhaps three hundred books on the topic of prayer. Classical books, contemporary books – books, books, and more books. My mind was swimming with all the definitions of prayer and all the debates about prayer.

I had gotten so lost in Teresa of Avila's *Interior Castle* that I didn't know which room was which!

I will never forget that July night. There I was in the library completely alone. Everyone had left hours ago. It was late. I had read too much, studied too much. I was experiencing overload. How in one book can anyone deal with all the intricacies and all of the difficulties of prayer? There was no way. I threw up my hands, ready to abandon the project.

Then something happened, something that even today, many years later, I have difficulty explaining. The only way I know how to describe it is that I "saw" something. What I saw was the heart of God, and the heart of God was an open wound of love. Then, as best as I can discern it, I heard the voice of the true Shepherd (not outwardly but inwardly) saying, "I do not want you to abandon the project. Instead, I want you to tell my people, tell my children, that my heart is broken. Their distance and preoccupation wounds me. Tell them, tell my children, to come home."

That was all. But it was enough. The word was so clear and so true to the human condition. You see, we have been in a far country. It's been a country of noise and hurry and crowds. It's been a country of climb and push and shove. And God is inviting you and me to come home: home to where we belong, home to that for which we were created, home to the loving heart of God.

Now, it was out of this experience that the book's title emerged: *Prayer: Finding the Heart's True Home.* And from this experience flowed the concept of the home as an extended metaphor for prayer. By means of the interactive relationship of prayer, God welcomes us into the living room of his heart, where we can put on old slippers and share freely. God welcomes us into the kitchen of his friendship, where chatter and batter mix in good fun. God welcomes us into the study of his wisdom, where we can grow and stretch and ask all the questions we want. God welcomes us into the dining room of his strength, where we can feast to our heart's delight. God welcomes us into the workshop of his creativity, where we can become "co-laborers" with him, working together to determine the outcome of events. And God welcomes us into the bedroom of his rest, where we can be vulnerable and free. This is the place of deepest intimacy, where we can know and be known to the fullest.

So why pray? Not out of obligation. Not out of a desire to "get" things from God. Not in the hopes of enhancing our standing in the religious community.

No, we pray because God in his amazing grace calls to us, seeks us out, and urges us to respond to a love that will not let us go. This is why we pray.

## The Nature of True Prayer

When Arnold writes about "true prayer" we know immediately what this is contrasted with. And while he is far too gentle to describe the opposite of true prayer in any detail, we have all been around "false prayer" long enough and often enough that we instinctively understand the contrast.

I'll concentrate on three major ideas. The first is that we come to experience prayer as the flow of a life. It is far too small a concept to think of prayer as a faucet that we can turn on and off at will. Rather, "It is the imbibing of life itself. If we stop praying, life ebbs away."

Some of us have come to speak of this reality as a "with-God" kind of life, and such a life is right at the heart of the work of prayer. In fact, the name *Immanuel,* meaning in Hebrew "God is with us," is the title given to the one and only Redeemer because it refers to God's everlasting intent for human life – namely, that we should in every aspect be a dwelling place of God. The wise apostle Paul reminds us that through Jesus "the whole structure is joined together and grows into a holy temple in the Lord; in whom you also are built together spiritually into a dwelling place for God" (Eph. 2:21–22).

We are meant to live "with-God." This dynamic, pulsating, with-God kind of life is on nearly every page of the Bible. To the point of redundancy we hear that God is *with* his people: with Abraham and Moses; with Esther and David; with Isaiah, Jeremiah, Amos, Micah, Haggai and Malachi; with Mary, Peter, James and John; with Paul and Barnabas; with Priscilla and Aquila; with Lydia, Timothy, Epaphroditus, and Phoebe; and with a host of others too numerous to name. God is *with* us, and it is by means of prayer that we are enabled to be *with* God. Here. Now. Continually.

The wonderful verse "Behold, I stand at the door and knock" (Rev. 3:20) was originally penned for believers, not unbelievers. Jesus is knocking at the door of our heart – daily, hourly, moment by moment. He is longing to eat with us, to commune with us. He desires a perpetual Eucharistic feast in the inner sanctuary of the soul. Jesus is knocking, knocking, knocking. Prayer opens the door. Arnold writes, "'Eating the flesh' and 'drinking the blood' of the Son of Man actually takes place every time we meet him personally, so that he is in us and we are in him."

The second major idea is that the Holy Spirit is the instrumental agent of all true prayer. Arnold writes, "When we pray let us remember that God in his Spirit approaches and calls us first." The Spirit initiates prayer, not us. When our prayers are little more than inarticulate groans and sighs, the Holy Spirit intercedes and interprets these yearnings before God for us (Rom. 8:26).

Arnold rightly makes much of this point: "Without the Holy Spirit there is no prayer in faith. There is not even faith." "God gives himself to us as the Holy Spirit." "Only in this river of the Spirit, flowing full of God's power, can faith live. Away from this river it dies like a fish on dry land."

The point being made here is that for prayer to be "true" something beyond us needs to occur. Something spiritual, something supernatural, something divine needs to happen. Upon this we humbly depend.

This leads us to the third major idea. If anything of genuine substance is to occur in prayer we need to learn to listen to the Lord. "For this reason," writes Arnold, "prayer is first listening to God." To underscore the importance of this listening he adds, "Not only individuals, but every church and fellowship that hopes to discover powerful, united prayer first needs to practice silence, for it is important that we learn to recognize what God wishes to say."

Some may wonder about naming this listening silence a "major idea." This is where we need to see the value of the hidden preparation through which God puts his people. Consider Moses in the desert, tucked away for year after silent year. "True silence," writes Catherine de Hueck Doherty, "is a key to the immense and flaming heart of God."[3]

The great spiritual writer François Fénelon counsels us, "Be silent, and listen to God. Let your heart be in such a state of preparation that his Spirit may impress upon you such virtues as will please him. Let all within you listen to him. This silence of all outward and earthly affection and of human thoughts within us is essential if we are to hear his voice."[4] Truly silence is a "major idea."

This stillness in the depths of our souls can have unusual results not just for us individually but as a community as well. Arnold observes, "Through the Spirit, we will become unanimous in silence. Meeting in silence, we will hear the same voice and perceive the same truth. So unity comes into being, unity of heart and of voice."

Ken Medema, a blind musician, was once at a retreat center where Carolynn and I used to live and where I wrote *Celebration of Discipline.* At this retreat center, Tilikum, Ken penned these simple words:

Teach me to stop and listen,
Teach me to center down.
Teach me the use of silence,
Teach me where peace is found.

Teach me to hear your calling,
Teach me to search your Word.
Teach me to hear in silence,
Things I have never heard.

Teach me to be collected.
Teach me to be in tune,
Teach me to be directed,
Silence will end so soon.

Then when it's time for moving,
Grant it that I might bring,
To every day and moment,
Peace from a silent spring.[5]

One of the most sterling witnesses to this reality comes from seventeenth-century theologian Robert Barclay. He happened upon a Quaker meeting for worship and graphically describes what occurred: "When I came into the silent assemblies of God's people, I felt a secret power among them, which touched my heart. And as I gave way to it, I found the evil in me weakening, and the good lifted up. Thus it was that I was knit into them and united with them. And I hungered more and more for the increase of this power and life until I could feel myself perfectly redeemed."[6]

Three major ideas: experiencing a with-God life; learning dependence on the Holy Spirit; entering a listening silence. Arnold concludes, "When we sincerely ask God for his Spirit, he comes and speaks and acts (Acts 4:31, 8:15–17). His divine energy is always present, ready to strike like lightning. But the only ground into which it can discharge its power is our humble, concentrated readiness in prayer."

### Does God Hear Us?

We now come to *the* question that every person who is learning to pray has asked and will ask again and again. And it is right here, and in the next section on the obstacles to prayer, that we receive Arnold's most detailed teaching on the three great movements in Christian prayer that I outlined earlier.

Providing an answer to the question of whether God hears us is both simple and complex. The simple answer is, "Yes, indeed, God hears us. Always!" Arnold begins by reminding us of the omnipresence of God. "God is always near," he writes, "near, very near."

"Near, very near." How important for us to know this teaching deep in the marrow of our bones. Many of us, when we recite the first line of the Lord's Prayer, "Our Father who art in heaven," are actually praying, "Our Father who art very far away from us!" But in Hebrew cosmology there are several heavens and the first heaven is literally the atmosphere around us. And so Jesus is teaching us to pray, "Our Father who art right in front of our noses . . ." Remember, Jesus promises never to leave us nor forsake us. God does indeed hear our prayers.

Now we come to the "complex" part in answering our question. By means of prayer God is inviting us into a living relationship with himself and he is slowly, step by step, helping us to bring our will into perfect alignment with his will. Remember, God's will is altogether right and good. Nine times in this section alone Arnold speaks to us of God's perfect will. But stubbornness, rebellion, and selfish desire keep us insisting on our own way, our own will, and this hinders our prayers. Remember, God never forces us to accept his will. The irresistible and the indisputable are the two things that God, by his very nature, will never use. No, God waits for us to choose the right and the good. And it is this freedom of choice, this freedom of will, that makes the answer to this question complex.

But even in our hard-hearted rebellion Arnold reminds us: "God wants to know what our will is." And he encourages us: "God is always ready. With the intensity of his holy will, he longs for people of faith to speak, pray, live, and believe so completely in the living Jesus that he is at last able to intervene and act as he has always wanted to act."

Another thing: Throughout this work of prayer we learn persistence, like the widow before the unjust judge in Jesus' parable (Luke 18:1–8). We experience "ardent longing" and "urgent desire." We learn to keep praying and not to give up. We even learn to "be ready to suffer godforsakenness, yet still pray trustingly, 'Father, into your hands I commit my spirit!' (Luke 23:46)." These are the lessons of persistence.

It has probably occurred to you that the question "Does God hear us?" carries with it a corresponding question: "Do we hear God?" Earlier we considered the importance of listening prayer if we are to hear from God. In addition, if we expect to hear from God we need to address the issue of the means God uses to speak to us.

God can, of course, speak to us in many ways; who can confine the Spirit of God? In the past God has spoken to his children by means of angels, visions, dreams, signs, and fleeces. More often God has used the Bible, or the wisdom of the Christian community, or simply a gentle nudging from the Spirit. Sometimes God will speak to us through the fireworks of a Mt. Sinai. More often God bypasses the earthquake, wind, and fire and instead comes to us by means of a "still small voice" (1 Kings 19:1–18).

Most important of all is the coming of Jesus as the fulfillment of the messianic hope for a prophet like Moses who will teach his people himself. As God promised Moses, "I will raise up for them a prophet like you from among their own people; I will put my words in the mouth of the prophet, who shall speak to them everything that I command" (Deut. 18:18). In fulfilling this messianic hope, Jesus closes the distance that had been created between human beings and God and once again brings the people into the intimate and immediate presence of God. Indeed, Jesus becomes the eternal mediator of the presence of God. The conversational relationship is restored.

As God's eschatological prophet, Jesus brings to full completion the great line of the prophets. The writer to the Hebrews declares, "Long ago God spoke to our ancestors in many and various ways by the prophets, but in these last days he has spoken to us by the Son" (Heb. 1:1–2). The practical difference is this: now our eternal, heavenly prophet speaks and teaches; we listen and obey. "Suddenly a bright cloud overshadowed them, and from the cloud a voice said, 'This is my Son, the Beloved; with him I am well pleased; *listen to him*'" (Matt. 17:5, emphasis added).

What does this mean? Instead of a scattered succession of prophets at irregular intervals, we have *the* eschatological prophet who is always in our midst. Instead of a written code of laws we have *the* living prophet who writes his laws on our hearts. Instead of a priestly temple religion we have *the* heavenly priest who is able to present his people to God without blemish.

So now, Jesus Christ is alive and here to teach his people himself. He has not contracted laryngitis. His voice is not hard to hear. His vocabulary is not difficult to understand. We can hear his voice and obey his word – today.

Just as we can distinguish between human speakers by the quality of their voice, the spirit in their voice, and the content of what is being said, so we can learn to recognize the voice of the true Shepherd. The quality of Jesus' voice is one of drawing and encouraging. The spirit in Jesus' voice is all grace and mercy. And the content of what Jesus says is always consistent with what we find in scripture – we have a huge biblical witness upon which to test our leadings.

### Obstacles to Prayer

In this section Arnold bears down hard on the central issue in the work of prayer – the transformation of the human personality. God intends for us to be so formed into the image of Christ that the natural outflow of our life is "love, joy, peace, patience, kindness, generosity, faithfulness, gentleness, and self-control" (Gal. 5:22–23). Paul writes, "I am in travail until Christ be formed in you" (Gal. 4:19). This is God's intent for you and for me. And prayer is one of the chief means for achieving this goal.[7]

C. S. Lewis declares, "The command 'Be ye perfect' is not idealistic gas. . . . God is going to make us into creatures that can obey that command. . . . If we let him – for we can prevent him if we choose – he will make the feeblest and filthiest of us into . . . a dazzling, radiant, immortal creature, pulsating all through with such energy and joy and wisdom and love as we cannot now imagine, a bright stainless mirror which reflects back to God perfectly (though, of course, on a smaller scale) his own boundless power and delight and goodness. The process will be long and in parts very painful; but that is what we are in for. Nothing less. He meant what he said."[8]

So, the most persistent obstacle to prayer is our untransformed self. God's will and way are not our will and way. Arnold states it rather strongly: "Our own nature is always interfering when God tries to reveal himself. Our personalities get in the way, because in each of us there are countless thoughts, feelings, and traits of character that are not completely centered on the kingdom of God or compatible with the spirit of Jesus. Every prayer is therefore inevitably burdened with personal mistakes and desires."

Arnold calls this struggle we have against the will of God by its proper name: sin. He especially (and rightly) focuses upon the "self" sins, such as self-esteem, self-justification, and self-importance.

It is easy to appreciate Arnold's passion here, especially given the historical context in which he wrote. But in pressing hard on the problem of sin he perhaps overstates his case. When he says that "sin and the prayer of faith exclude each other," or that "God dwells only in hearts that have been completely purified," I am concerned that these expressions can be taken in unfortunate directions.

Maybe it is simply a matter of emphasis. When people ask me if God will answer a sinner's prayer, I will often answer in jest, "He better or we will all be in trouble!" But in all seriousness, it is important to underscore that God is with us even in our stubbornness and rebellion.

We often say that a little child can never draw a bad picture. Well, maybe a child of God cannot utter a bad prayer. You see, we come to God with our egocentric, greed-motivated prayers and God says, "That's my child who has chosen to be with me. It is a good prayer and I will make it an even better prayer." How? Well, by lovingly transforming us into better persons.

Arnold stresses that the excessive individualism of our culture is another obstacle to a life of prayer. He writes, "Our prayers remain insipid if their primary focus is on our personal needs." His concern here is the community life of the people of God. "In praying to God . . . we can overcome the human resistance of our rebellious 'I' only through the 'we' of the church."

The first thing we need to stress when we speak of the Christian community is that it is formed by Jesus and lives its life through Jesus. Jesus teaches us what is right and what is wrong and gives us the power to do the right and reject the wrong. Jesus is the one who gathers us into a community of faith, which learns together, prays together, obeys together, and suffers together.

Jesus himself is the builder of this new community, this *ecclesia*. For God's gathered community the central question is, "Are we living in the life and power in which the apostles lived?" If we have this, nothing else is needed. If we lack this, nothing else will suffice.

The gathered Christian community does not come about by building up a human-made religious organization but by our responding to the call of our heavenly Prophet who brings us together into a loving, conversational relationship with God and with one another. Together we become the friends of Jesus; "You are my friends if you do what I command you" (John 15:14).

## Praying for the Kingdom

It is moving to think of Arnold penning this final section as Europe stood on the brink of the First World War. Since he is here teaching on the Lord's Prayer as the model for our praying for the kingdom, he has to deal with the subject of forgiveness ("forgive us our sins as we forgive those who have sinned against us"). Does he anticipate the horrors of the turbulent years ahead as he calls us to follow the example of Jesus on the cross and "pray most of all for those who have hurt us"? He also urges prayer for the kingdom of God to "encompass the whole world." "Our personal prayers remain selfish unless they are placed in the larger context of God's rulership being established on earth."

Prayer of this kind is no pious exercise for the devout. No, all true prayer will push us into the real world of pain and suffering, sorrow and anguish. Love of God, of necessity, leads us to love of neighbor. They are not two commands, but one. Our prayer involves work for justice and peace, work for mercy and compassion. This is no abstraction, but a real working among the bruised and broken of the world. This is how we pray for God's kingdom to come and God's will to be done on earth as it is in heaven.

This is not work in our own strength but through the power of the Spirit. The surest sign that what we are doing is a cooperative work *with* God is that the results are far in excess of the labor we put in. Arnold says it best, "When we call on God, we are asking him to do something that we cannot, to bring into being something that we ourselves do not know how to create. We are seeking for the impossible to happen, for something to be changed irrevocably that we could never change. We are asking for a history to unfold for which we ourselves could never be responsible."

Perhaps no one can ever satisfactorily answer the questions we have considered: Why pray? What is true prayer? Does God hear us when we pray? What obstacles do we face in seeking to pray? How do we pray for Christ's kingdom to come upon the earth? But as we continue to think about each of these questions in the context of ordinary life, we are learning to burn the perpetual flame of devotion upon the altar of God's love. ✦

1. See Thomas R. Kelly, *A Testament of Devotion* (New York: HarperOne, 1996).

2. See Richard J. Foster, *Prayer: Finding the Heart's True Home* (San Francisco: HarperSanFrancisco, 1992).

3. Catherine de Hueck Doherty, *Poustinia: Christian Spirituality of the East for Western Man* (Notre Dame, IN: Ave Maria Press, 1983), 21.

4. François Fénelon as quoted in Foster, *Prayer: Finding the Heart's True Home,* 163.

5. Ken Medema, "Teach Me to Stop," *Teach Me to Stop (and Listen)* (Waco, TX: Word Music, 1978).

6. *Barclay's Apology in Modern English,* ed. Dean Freiday (Manasquan, NJ: Sowers, 1980), 254.

7. Prayer is one of a well-known list of spiritual disciplines that are meant to help us to "train [ourselves] in godliness" (1 Tim 4:7). I tend to think of prayer as the most basic of the disciplines of engagement (as opposed to the disciplines of abstinence) because it draws us into an ongoing, interactive communication with God in the course of daily life. For further discussion of these matters see Richard J. Foster, *Celebration of Discipline: The Path to Spiritual Growth* (San Francisco: HarperSanFrancisco, 1998) and Dallas Willard, *The Spirit of the Disciplines: Understanding How God Changes Lives* (San Francisco: Harper & Row, 1988).

8. C. S. Lewis, *Mere Christianity* (New York: HarperCollins, 2001), 205–206.

## Related Titles from Plough

**Cries from the Heart:** *Stories of Struggle and Hope*

JOHANN CHRISTOPH ARNOLD

True stories of real men and women who overcame adversity and found healing and inner peace through turning to God in prayer.

**Evening Prayers:** *For Every Day of the Year*

CHRISTOPH FRIEDRICH BLUMHARDT

These prayers bespeak a certainty in God's nearness. The peace that flows from them comes from an unshakeable conviction that God's kingdom is indeed on the way.

**Why We Live in Community**

EBERHARD ARNOLD AND THOMAS MERTON

In this time-honored manifesto Arnold and Merton join the vital discussion of what community is all about: a great adventure of faith shared with others.

**Discipleship:** *Living for Christ in the Daily Grind*

J. HEINRICH ARNOLD

A trusted pastor's guidance on topics such as surrender, forgiveness, purity, family life, community, leadership, and suffering.

Plough Publishing House
**www.plough.com**
1-800-521-8011 ♦ 845-572-3455
PO BOX 398 ♦ Walden, NY 12586 ♦ USA

Brightling Rd ♦ Robertsbridge ♦ East Sussex TN32 5DR ♦ UK
4188 Gwydir Highway ♦ Elsmore, NSW 2360 ♦ Australia